ENGAGE

A Guide to Enhancing Your Ministry Through Smarter Digital Outreach

© 2025 eCatholic. All Rights Reserved.

All rights reserved. No part of this work may be reproduced, transmitted or stored in any form whatsoever, printed or electronic, without prior written permission of the publisher.

ISBN: 979-8291609705 (paperback)

"Follow me, and I will make you fishers of men."

Matthew 4:19

CONTENTS

Preface
5

Chapter 1: Get To Know Your Online Flock
7

Chapter 2: Connect With Your Community
17

Chapter 3: Essentials of Effective (Online) Communication
22

Chapter 4: How to Craft Messaging That Inspires Action
31

Chapter 5: The Digital Evangelist Toolkit
35

Chapter 6: Multiply Your Message With Micro-Content
45

Chapter 7: Turn Clicks Into Fellowship
50

Chapter 8: Evaluating the Impact of Your Digital Ministry
52

Chapter 9: Navigating the Challenges of Evangelizing Online
57

Chapter 10: Where Do We Go From Here?
62

Preface

If you're reading this, you're probably wearing a dozen different hats right now. Youth minister, bulletin editor, web administrator, communications director...sound familiar? And now, on top of everything else, you're trying to figure out this whole "online presence" thing, and it's starting to give you a little bit of heartburn.

Let's face it: the internet isn't just a fad (if we haven't already noticed). It's where your parishioners–and the wider community–hang out these days. Whether you're a bustling parish or a small rural church, your online voice has the power to reach souls far beyond your own church walls.

But here's the thing: posting messages online, whether on your website, through email, or on social media, isn't about aimlessly casting your message into the void to see what sticks. It's about connecting, engaging, and, ultimately, leading souls to an encounter with Jesus Christ in this brave new digital world. Scary? Maybe a little. Exciting? You betcha!

Whether you consider yourself a total "newbie" or already feel confident when it comes to evangelizing online, then we've written this guide with you in mind. We'll walk you through the basics of how to effectively evangelize online and the digital tools to help you get there. And if you're more experienced, you'll still find practical tips, helpful reminders, and a few hidden gems along the way. From knowing your audience to crafting messages that really resonate to measuring your impact (and no, we don't just mean counting likes), this book will help you take your ministry to the next level.

If you're ready to elevate your online engagement and connect with your community like never before, then let's dive in!

Chapter 1
Get to Know Your Online Flock

*"For as in one body we have many members,
so we, though many, are one body in Christ."*
— *Romans 12:4-5*

Picture yourself at your parish's annual fall festival. When you arrive, to your left, you see a group of teens huddled around a smartphone, laughing at the latest TikTok craze. Nearby, a couple is snapping photos for the parish Instagram account, making sure to capture all the smiles, the beautiful decorations, and the fellowship. Off in the corner, Father Murphy is encouraging some of the older members to join the parish's email newsletter, with his trademark warmth and smile. Meanwhile, across the way, a lively group of young adults are deep in conversation and sharing highlights from the latest episode of their favorite podcast.

This scene illustrates the diverse landscape we're navigating in our ministry today. Just as you wouldn't use the same approach for each of these groups at the festival, your online communication strategy needs to be equally adaptable.

Understanding and connecting with your audience

is essential in order to effectively evangelize, whether it's in person, on your website, through social media, or even email or text message. Tailoring your approach to fit the unique characteristics of different groups is important. Just as we would adapt our tone to communicate with a lively group of teenagers, engage a women's Bible study with reflective discussions, or share practical insights with a men's fellowship, it's important to personalize our outreach to resonate with the diverse members of our community.

One effective way to achieve this is by creating what's called personas. Persona building is a popular strategy used by marketers to create detailed profiles that represent different segments of their audience. They help you understand the needs, preferences, and behaviors of each group, allowing you to tailor your content and engagement strategies accordingly. For example, you might create a persona for "Tommy Teenager," who loves short, engaging videos and interactive content, and another for "Busy Parent Patricia," who values informative, quick-read posts that fit into her hectic schedule. Each persona represents a particular demographic you serve in your parish.

By developing these personas, you can ensure that your messages are relevant and engaging for each segment of your audience. It's like having a roadmap that guides you in creating content that speaks directly to the hearts and minds of your community members.

Let's take a closer look at the types of audience personas you'll likely encounter in your online community and some of the best ways to reach them:

The Digital Natives
(Gen Z & Millennials)

This group was practically born with smartphones in their hands. They can be remarkably creative and love to scroll through content quickly. They're all about quick, visual content that grabs their attention and keeps them engaged. This generation is skilled at multitasking and consuming information rapidly, so your messages need to stand out in a crowded digital space.

The key to this group is to keep it short, authentic, and impactful. In a world of quick scrolls and shorter attention spans, it's important to get to the point quickly and make every second count. Authenticity is crucial—they value genuine, relatable content over highly polished productions. Don't be afraid to show the real, human side of your ministry. And yes, it's okay to use emojis! Emojis add a visual element to your message and can convey emotions or highlight key points in a way that words alone can't.

They make your content feel more approachable and relatable. Just be mindful not to overdo it—use emojis to enhance your message, not overshadow it.

Here are some content ideas to help you engage this group:

> **Trendy challenges and hashtags (#)**
> Participate in popular TikTok challenges or create your own Catholic faith-based challenge.

Encourage young parishioners to join in and use a unique hashtag (e.g., #FaithInActionChallenge) to create a sense of community and shared mission. Hashtags are a way to not simply categorize your posts, but is a way of telling the "algorithm" what your video is about so that it will help connect your content with the right audience.

Influencer collaborations
Partner with young Catholic influencers in your community and online who can help spread your message. Their endorsement can lend credibility and reach to your content, making it more appealing to younger audiences.

Virtual hangouts and Bible studies
Use platforms like Instagram Live to host virtual hangouts or Bible study sessions, creating a relaxed space where young people can connect, discuss their faith, and ask questions. For example, your pastor could invite followers to an AMA (Ask Me Anything) session during regular office hours and engage with viewers in real time. This approach not only makes priests more accessible but also encourages those who may not typically reach out to take that first step. While questions in the chat should be vetted before responding, the pastor can personally acknowledge participants and even invite them to schedule an in-person or phone appointment for deeper discussions.

Creative video series
Develop a short, creative video series that explains church teaching, share personal testimonies, or highlight parish activities. For example, "60 Second Bible Study with Father John" can be a weekly series where the priest shares quick reflections or answers questions about specific passages in scripture.

> **Podcast recommendations**
> Share recommendations for Catholic podcasts or your own parish's podcast. This group often listens to podcasts during commutes or workouts, making it a convenient way to engage with faith content.

> **Daily inspiration and challenges**
> Create daily or weekly inspiration posts with challenges that encourage young people to live out their faith. For example, "Monday Motivation: Say a prayer for someone who needs it today" or "Friday Faith Challenge: Share a Bible verse that inspires you."

> **Engage with popular trends**
> Keep an eye on trending topics and viral content. Adapt these trends in a way that aligns with your parish's mission and values, making your content timely and relevant.

Preferred platforms

 TikTok    Instagram    X (formerly Twitter)

 YouTube Shorts    LinkedIn

The Tech-Savvy (Gen X)

This group is comfortable with technology but appreciates both digital and traditional communication. They grew up during the rise of the internet and are pretty well-versed in navigating various platforms, along with email and texting. Facebook is often their go-to social platform, although on occasion you may find some reading the headlines on X. They value content that is informative, engaging, and sometimes nostalgic—such as references to the early days of the internet, memorable cultural moments from the 80s and 90s, or significant events in Church history that they may recall from their youth. Mixing it up with longer posts, short videos, and interactive content will keep them engaged and coming back for more.

Here are some content ideas to reach this group:

> **Informative articles and blog posts**
> Write blog posts on your parish website about relevant topics such as understanding the Mass, the significance of the sacraments, or reflections on the lives of the saints. Share these posts on Facebook with captivating headlines and inviting comments for further discussion.

> **Nostalgic content**
> Share throwback photos or stories from past parish events, missions, or milestones. Nostalgic content can resonate deeply with this group, reminding them of their own faith journeys and experiences within the Church.

> **Live stream events and webinars**
> Host live stream events, such as Q&A sessions with the pastor, virtual Bible studies, or webinars on relevant Catholic topics. This interactive format allows for real-time engagement and fosters a sense of connection.

> **Email newsletters**
> Keep them informed with regular email newsletters that include upcoming events, reflections, and parish news. Segment your email list to tailor content to specific interests, ensuring that everyone receives information relevant to them.

Preferred platforms

Facebook   X (formerly Twitter)   LinkedIn   YouTube   Email   Texting

The Digital Adopters
(Baby Boomers)

This group is increasingly online, particularly on Facebook. They appreciate more detailed content and don't mind longer reads. They value depth, meaning, and a sense of community. Sharing fuller versions of your homilies or deep dives into faith topics will resonate well with them. They appreciate thoughtful and substantial content that enriches their understanding and practice of the faith.

Here are some content ideas to reach this group:

> **Extended homilies and reflections**
> Post the full text or videos of homilies on your parish website and share them. Accompany these with brief introductions or summaries to entice them to read or watch the full content.

Deep dives into faith topics
Write in-depth articles or blog posts on significant aspects of Catholic teaching or Church history. Topics like the Eucharist or the lives of the saints can provide the rich content they crave.

Prayer and devotional resources
Provide resources for personal prayer and devotion, such as downloadable prayer guides, novenas, or rosary meditations. Regularly share these resources on your website and social media.

Preferred platforms

Facebook   X (formerly Twitter)   LinkedIn
YouTube   Email

The Tech-Hesitant
(The Silent Generation)

Yes, they do exist, and yes, they matter too! These individuals might need a little extra help and encouragement to get involved online. They may not be as at ease with technology but are open to learning, especially when it improves their connection to the parish or helps to enrich their faith. Providing clear, step-by-step instructions for accessing online content and offering hands-on support can make a significant difference.

Here are some creative ways to reach this group:

- **Step-by-step guides**
  Create simple, easy-to-follow guides on how to use various digital platforms and tools. Use clear language and include plenty of screenshots or diagrams. Share these guides in print form at church and digitally via email and your parish website.

- **One-on-one tech support**
  Offer personalized tech support. Have tech-savvy parish volunteers available to assist individuals one-on-one with setting up accounts, navigating websites, or using digital devices.

- **Interactive kiosks**
  Set up interactive kiosks at church where parishioners can access digital content with the help of volunteers. This can be a stepping stone for those hesitant to try it on their own.

- **Printed materials**
  Provide printed versions of important content, such as newsletters, event calendars, and sermon transcripts. Make these available at church for those who prefer traditional media but also include information on how to access the same content online.

Preferred platforms

Traditional Print   Facebook   Email

Keep in mind that your online presence is not just for your parish family, but also a powerful tool for reaching those who might never set foot inside your church. It's important to be mindful of who else might be in your digital congregation without you even knowing it:

The Unchurched Seekers
These individuals are curious about faith but might feel intimidated by the idea of walking into a church. Your online content could be their first step towards faith. Create welcoming content that addresses common questions. Consider developing or sharing great content that already exists from trusted Catholic sources, such as "Catholicism 101" or "What to Expect at Mass" guides.

Fallen Away Catholics
In our communities, we have members who have fallen away and no longer practice their Catholic faith. However, that doesn't necessarily mean they've lost interest. Use live streaming for Masses and events, and invite them to tune in. It's a great way to re-engage this group that has wandered off the beaten path.

The Wider Community
Your online voice can reach Catholics (and non-Catholics alike) far beyond your parish boundaries. Share what makes your parish unique, whether it's your amazing choir, vibrant multicultural ministry, or legendary Lenten fish fry. Let your parish personality shine! You never know what might be the hook that draws them in.

Getting to know your online flock isn't about putting people in boxes. It's like being a good host at a party – the more you know about your guests, the better you can make them feel welcome and engaged. So, take a moment to think about who's in your online community. Doing so will empower you to create impactful content that your audience finds useful.

Chapter 2
Connect with Your Community

"Let us consider how to stir up one another to love and good works, encouraging one another." — *Hebrews 10:24-25*

Imagine you've just crafted what you think is the perfect message. You hit "post" and…crickets. Sound familiar? Don't worry, you're not alone! Welcome to the exciting (and sometimes confusing) world of online ministry, where connecting with your audience is both an art and a science.

But here's the million-dollar question: How do you make those connections feel as warm and genuine as the "sign of peace" at Sunday Mass?

Your journey as a digital evangelist might often feel like Indiana Jones meets Mr. Rogers—exploring uncharted territories while building a friendly community—but there's nothing more effective at generating engagement than authenticity. Authenticity is about being true to who you are and what your parish community represents. It's about showing the genuinely human, everyday moments that make your community special.

Authenticity is the Message

You know that feeling when someone's trying too hard to impress or is simply being insincere? It's like watching a commercial that feels too polished and disconnected from reality.

Authenticity is key, especially online. You don't have to be the trendiest or most polished communicator. People crave genuine connections and relatable stories. By staying true to your identity and what your parish represents, you'll nurture trust and strengthen your community. To help you establish this level of authenticity and trust with your followers, here are just a few ways to do that a little more effectively:

> **People love a peek behind the curtain**
> Share photos of your parish team setting up for events or your priest's desk covered in homily notes. It humanizes your ministry and makes people feel like insiders. Show the everyday moments that make your parish unique—preparing for a community picnic, choir members rehearsing for an upcoming concert, or your youth group packing care kits for the homeless. These glimpses make your community feel more connected and involved. Whether it's a short video of volunteers planting flowers in the church garden, or a snapshot of families participating in a parish clean-up day, these behind-the-scenes moments invite your audience to experience parts of parish life they hardly ever get to see. By showcasing these human aspects, you create a relatable and welcoming online presence that fosters a deeper sense of community and belonging.

- **Let personalities shine**
  Your parish isn't just a building; it's the people. Let their unique voices come through in your content. Maybe Father Jim has a quirky sense of humor that really connects with people, or Sister Mary is a whiz at explaining complex theology. Highlighting these personalities makes your content more relatable and engaging. Consider sharing short interviews, personal stories, or even day-in-the-life videos of your parish staff and volunteers. When your community sees the authentic, personal side of those who serve, it deepens their connection and trust.

- **Address real issues**
  Don't shy away from talking about the challenges Catholics face in daily life. Your online space can be a place for honest conversations about living the faith in today's world. Whether it's dealing with stress, finding time for prayer, or navigating moral dilemmas, addressing these topics head-on shows that the Church is a relevant and supportive community. Use your platform to discuss real issues, provide spiritual guidance, and offer a place for people to share their struggles and triumphs. This not only shows empathy and understanding but also provides practical support and inspiration.

Empathy is the Heartbeat

In the fast-paced world of online communications, where everyone is seeking attention, empathy often gets overlooked. Yet, empathy—the ability to understand

and share the feelings of others—is a powerful tool for creating meaningful connections. In the context of parish life, empathy is about showing compassion, understanding, and support for your community members, recognizing their joys, struggles, and needs, and responding in a way that makes them feel heard and valued. Empathy is the heartbeat of your ministry, both online and in-person.

Here are some ways to weave it into your content:

- **Listen to your followers**
  Before crafting a single message, take the time to listen to your community. What are their concerns, questions, and joys? Use social media polls, comment sections, and direct messages to gather insights. When people see that you're genuinely interested in their lives, they're more willing to engage with you.

- **Acknowledge and address their struggles**
  Life is full of ups and downs, and your parishioners are no exception. Use your platform to acknowledge the challenges they face, whether it's the stress of daily life, grief from losing a loved one, or the anxiety of uncertain times. Share content that offers comfort, support, and hope. For instance, a post about finding peace in prayer during stressful times, or a video from the pastor offering words of encouragement for the week, can resonate deeply with those who might be going through a rough patch.

ⓘ Celebrate the joys and milestones

Empathy isn't just about addressing difficulties; it's also about sharing in the joy and celebrating milestones. Highlight birthdays, anniversaries, baptisms, and other special events within your parish. A simple congratulatory message or a shout-out in the parish newsletter or on social media can make people feel as though they're part of a larger family–and indeed, they are!

As St. Paul reminded the early Christians in the Church of Rome (Rom. 12:15): "Rejoice with those who rejoice; mourn with those who mourn." This captures the essence of transforming the often impersonal online experience into a chance to create meaningful personal connections. By sharing in the joys and sorrows of your community, you'll open doors to evangelization and deeper relationships you never thought possible. When people feel understood and supported, they're more likely to engage, connect, and grow in their faith with your community. Empathy transforms your online presence from just another online profile into a lifeline of support that allows the loving gaze of Christ to shine through.

Chapter 3
Essentials of Effective (Online) Communication

"Let your speech always be gracious, seasoned with salt, so that you may know how you ought to answer each person." — *Colossians 4:6*

Alright, now let's discuss the secret sauce for your online messaging. Don't worry—it's not as complicated as interpreting the IRS tax code (thank goodness!). These core principles will help you craft messages that speak directly to your members and resonate with them.

When Jesus spoke in parables, he wasn't trying to confuse people; He was making complex ideas simple and relatable. That's your mission online. By following these steps, you can create clear, engaging, and impactful content that brings your community closer together and strengthens their faith.

 Keep it simple

Imagine you're explaining your message to a busy mom wrangling three kids. If she can't grasp it in 30 seconds or less, simplify. Attention spans are short, and your audience is often multitasking. Break down your messages into bite-sized pieces, use clear and concise language, and focus on one main idea per post. Simplicity ensures your message is accessible and memorable.

2. **Avoid "churchy" jargon at first**
Unless you're writing for a theology conference, skip the fancy terms. "Transubstantiation" might not fly on Facebook, but "Jesus is truly present in the Eucharist" will. Keep in mind, you've got a diverse crowd you're speaking to, many who are well-formed in their faith and others who simply go through the motions. The key here is not to water down your messaging, but to make it approachable to as many as possible. Use plain language that conveys the beauty and depth of our faith in a way that's understandable to everyone. As the maxim of the great Jesuit missionaries says: "Enter through their door; lead them through yours." This approach to content creation helps bridge gaps in understanding and invites more people into deeper, more meaningful conversations about their faith.

3. **Use visual aids**
As the old saying goes, a picture is worth a thousand words, especially when you're trying to explain the Trinity! Infographics, photos, and videos are powerful tools for making complex ideas more digestible. Visual aids can capture attention quickly, illustrate your points more effectively, and make your content more engaging. For example, create an infographic that explains the key elements of the Mass or a short video that walks through the steps of a traditional prayer. These visual elements can help demystify

complex topics and make your content worth sharing.

Consistency is Key (But Don't Be Boring)

Just picture the Gospel of Mark suddenly taking a delightful Dr. Seuss-style rhyme halfway through. Quite the head-scratcher, right? Consistency in your messaging helps build trust and boost brand recognition online. By maintaining a steady and reliable presence, you create a sense of stability and familiarity for your audience.

 Develop a 'voice' for your parish: Is your intended approach to be warm and friendly? Inspirational and uplifting? Choose a tone that fits your parish personality and stick with it. Your voice should reflect the unique character of your parish community. Whether it's casual and conversational or more formal and reverent, consistency in your tone helps create a recognizable and trustworthy presence online. This consistent voice reassures your audience that they are engaging with a reliable source.

 Create a content calendar: Plan your posts around the liturgical calendar, ministry activity schedule, or school event calendar. Your followers should know they can count on you for Advent reflections or Lenten challenges. Keeping a content calendar will also help reduce the guesswork and allow you to think more strategically about your messaging each month.

⨯ **Mix it up:** Consistency doesn't have to mean monotony. Throw your audience a surprise every now and then, like maybe a video travel log from Father Mike's recent pilgrimage to Rome or scenes from the diocesan Eucharistic Congress.

Don't be afraid to mix up your regular posts with unexpected content such as live "office hours" with Father, a random raffle giveaway, or spotlight features on different parish ministries. These surprises can spark renewed interest and engagement, making your online presence feel dynamic and lively.

Engage, Don't Just Broadcast

Your online presence should not be viewed as a digital pulpit but rather more like a virtual parish hall. Conversation and community happen on a two-way street. Whether it's through social media, your website, or email newsletters, engaging in back-and-forth communication helps transform your online interactions from mere announcements into meaningful connections. For example, on your website, include a comment section on blog posts where parishioners can share their thoughts and ask questions. In your email newsletters, encourage recipients to reply with their own stories or prayer requests.

To create a more engaging online presence, it's essential that we move beyond the random approach of simply "shooting in the dark" to see what sticks. Here are some practical ways to inspire more meaningful interactions:

Ask questions: Let's ignite meaningful conversations by starting with thought-provoking questions. How about prompting discussions with questions like, "Have you ever wondered why the Church teaches XYZ?" or "What family traditions do you cherish most during Advent/Lent?" Questions like these create an inviting space for everyone to share their unique thoughts, experiences, and insights. This not only boosts engagement but also provides invaluable insights into the beliefs and practices of your community. It serves as a litmus test to identify areas that could benefit from a little pastoral attention or affirm the areas where your community is thriving. These thoughtful questions have the power to deepen our parish family's understanding of their faith and strengthen their relationship with the Lord and with each other.

Respond promptly: If someone comments on your post, don't leave them hanging. A quick reply shows you're listening and that you care. Acknowledging comments and engaging in conversation is often one of the reasons why most digital outreach falls flat on its face. Quick responses demonstrate that you value their participation. Whether it's a simple "thank you" or a more detailed response to a question or comment, your promptness helps foster a supportive and interactive online environment.

Create interactive content: Polls, quizzes, or "Fill in the blank" posts can boost engagement. For example, "My favorite part of being Catholic is ____" can spark some interesting discussions! Interactive content invites your audience to actively participate rather than passively react or consume information. Use polls to help you gather opinions on parish activities, quizzes to educate and entertain, and fill-in-the-blank posts to encourage personal sharing.

Pro Tip: Set aside time each day for online community management. It's like online office hours for your parish! It's a way to show that the same level of care they receive in person at the parish will be equally reflected in your community online.

Always Bring It Back to Your Mission

At the end of the day, we're not just chasing likes and shares. We're spreading the Good News of Jesus Christ to all who will listen. Don't underestimate the effectiveness of your message, and always think of the person on the other end. What message do you want them to hear? Are they ready to hear that message? What action would you like them to take, or how would you like to get them engaged in your parish? Keeping your mission front-and-center ensures that your online presence is not just noise but a meaningful extension of your ministry in the parish.

- **Link to deeper content:** Use your social media to drive people to more substantial content on your website, such as a special message from the pastor, a new video series from Word on Fire, or an invitation to an upcoming parish mission. Social media is an excellent starting point for engagement, while linking followers to deeper, more meaningful content on your website. By linking to these resources, you provide a pathway for your audience to explore their faith more deeply and become more involved in parish life.

- **Highlight your impact:** Share stories of how your parish is making a difference in the community. What new ministries have evolved as a result of greater parishioner engagement? Highlighting these stories not only demonstrates the impact of your parish's work but also inspires others to get involved. When people see the tangible outcomes of your mission, they're more likely to feel connected and motivated to give back in a way that they feel called.

 Invite participation: Every post should have a purpose. Whether it's joining a prayer group, volunteering at the food bank, or attending an upcoming event, give people a way to act on what they've just read. Clear calls to action guide your audience on how they can get involved and make a difference.

There's a reason why the scriptures are ripe with gardening and farming analogies. Just as seeds need time to grow and bear fruit, evangelization requires patience and nurturing. In order for people to be ready for the message, there needs to be a period of building trust and forming relationships. Think of Jesus' interaction with the woman at the well. He didn't start with a sermon or a rebuke; instead, He began with a simple, sincere conversation. He asked for a drink of water, listened to her story, and engaged with her in a way that showed genuine interest and care. Through this interaction, He built a connection and established trust, which then opened her heart to receive His message about living water and eternal life.

In our digital ministry, we can take a similar approach. Before we can share the profound truths of our Catholic faith, we need to first establish a relationship. This involves listening to people's stories, understanding their needs and concerns, and showing that we genuinely care about them as individuals. Just like a gardener tending to plants, we must cultivate these relationships with patience, consistency, and love.

Creating content that resonates on a personal level, responding thoughtfully to comments and messages, and engaging in meaningful conversations are all ways to build these relationships online. By taking the time to build these connections, we lay the groundwork for deeper spiritual engagement and growth, just as Jesus did with the woman at the well.

 Pro Tip: *End each post with a question or call to action. It could be as simple as "How will you put this into practice today?" Other examples may include, "What does this scripture mean to you?" or "Share a time when you experienced God's grace in your life." These prompts not only encourage engagement but also invite your community to reflect and participate actively in the conversation.*

Chapter 4

How to Craft Messaging That Inspires Action

"Each of you should use whatever gifts you have received to serve others, as faithful stewards of God's grace in its various forms." — 1 Peter 4:10

It's time to roll up those sleeves and dive into the nitty-gritty of content creation. Don't worry – you don't need to be the next Archbishop Fulton Sheen to make this work. With a few tips and tricks, you'll be crafting content that'll have your flock coming back faster than you can say, "Amen!" It just takes a little bit of practice and an ounce of wit to get it just right.

Sometimes, the best way to learn is through examples. That's why we've curated three sample messages to demonstrate how you can elevate an ordinary communication into one that is relatable, conversational, and exudes warmth and charm.

Example 1: Announcing a Parish Event

- ❌ **Original message:** The annual parish picnic will be held on Saturday, June 15th at 12 PM in the church parking lot. Please bring a dish to share.

✅ **Engaging message:** Calling all foodies and fellowship lovers! 🍽️ 🙌 Join us for our 'Loaves & Fishes Feast' (aka the annual parish picnic) on Saturday, June 15th at 12 PM. We're transforming our parking lot into a community banquet hall! Bring your favorite dish to share and let's break bread together. 🍞 RSVP on our website or after Mass this Sunday. Can't wait to see you there!

What makes this message better?
- Uses engaging, friendly language
- A catchy event name attracts attention
- Incorporates humor and emojis for visual appeal
- Provides a clear call-to-action (RSVP)
- Creates excitement and anticipation

Example 2: Promoting a Ministry

❌ **Original message:** The St. Vincent de Paul Society meets every Tuesday at 7 PM in the parish hall. New volunteers are welcome.

✅ **Engaging message:** Want to be the hands and feet of Christ in our community? 🙌 Our St. Vincent de Paul team is looking for everyday superheroes to join the mission! We meet every Tuesday at 7 PM in the parish hall to plan our next moves in service to the less fortunate of our community. No cape required – just bring your heart and willingness to serve. Bonus: We'll have cookies & light refreshments! 🍪

Learn more about how you can make a difference at [insert link to online sign-up form].

What makes this message better?
- Uses inspiring language that connects to faith
- Incorporates a touch of humor
- Clearly states the purpose of the ministry
- Provides a specific time and place
- Includes a call-to-action with a link for more information

Example 3: Sharing a Scripture Reflection

❌ **Original message:** Today's Gospel is from Matthew 5:14-16. Jesus tells us to let our light shine before others.

✅ **Engaging message:** "You are the light of the world." - Matthew 5:14. 🕯️ Ever feel like you're just a tiny candle in a world of darkness? Jesus reminds us that even the smallest light can pierce the deepest darkness. Today, let's talk about practical ways to let the light of Christ shine through us:

😄 Smile at a stranger
🗣️ Offer a word of encouragement
🤗 Perform a random act of kindness

How will you shine the light of Christ today to those around you? Share your ideas in the comments below! ⬇️

What makes this message better?
- Provides the full scripture quote for context
- Relates the scripture to everyday life
- Offers practical application points
- Encourages interaction and sharing
- Uses emojis to add visual interest

The goal isn't to be flashy or water down the message. It's about presenting the message in a way that's understandable and resonates with people. Your content should connect with your audience's everyday experiences. Speak their language: if you're targeting young adults, consider using references that are relevant to their current interests and contexts. Address the real issues they face, like balancing faith and work or raising Catholic children in a secular world. Not sure what your community needs or what type of content speaks to them? Try embedding a simple form on your website to collect feedback. After all, your website isn't just a digital bulletin board; it's the foundation of your parish's digital engagement.

Chapter 5
The Digital Evangelist Toolkit

"Go into all the world and preach the gospel to all creation." — Mark 16:15

St. Paul was a master communicator, harnessing the tools of his time to engage with various communities, share the Gospel, and establish the early Church. Today, we are blessed with even more powerful (digital) tools at our fingertips, from websites, email, and text messaging to social media and live streaming, that can help us reach people even beyond our church walls.

In this chapter, we want to provide a high-level overview of the digital tools at your disposal, and help you think differently about how to use each tool thoughtfully and effectively:

Websites

Think of your website as your virtual parish hall—it's where people come to get information, connect with friends, and be inspired to deepen their faith. The key to a great parish website is keeping content fresh, easy to navigate, and mobile-responsive. Imagine a potential visitor trying to find your Mass times on their phone while running errands.

If they can't find that information in a few quick taps on their smartphone, you might miss out on welcoming a new face on Sunday morning. And remember, your website isn't just for newcomers—it's for your regular parishioners too. Make sure they can easily find what they need, whether it's the latest bulletin, the Religious Ed sign-up form, or online giving options. Your website is a gateway to everything your parish has to offer, so it's mission critical that the information you post is relevant, up-to-date, and can be accessed quickly.

> **KEY TAKEAWAYS**
>
> **❯ Keep content fresh**
> Regularly update your website with the latest news, events, and resources to keep visitors coming back.
>
> **❯ Easy to use**
> Ensure your website is easy to navigate, with clear menus and quick access to essential information.
>
> **❯ Mobile-responsive**
> Make sure your site can be easily viewed from any device, as most of your visitors will likely access it from their smartphones.

Social Media

Just as Jesus went to where the people were, we need to be present where our community spends their time online. But don't feel like you need to be everywhere at once. It's better to do a great job on one or two platforms than to spread yourself thin trying to manage them all.

Let's briefly explore some of the influential platforms today and how we can approach them in the best way possible:

Facebook is like the town square of the internet. It's perfect for sharing a mix of content, from daily scripture reflections to photos from your latest parish picnic or special Masses with the bishop. You can even create private groups for more in-depth discussions or to coordinate ministry activities. And don't forget about Facebook Live—it's a great way to broadcast Mass, special events or even host Q&A sessions about the faith with your pastor.

How often should you post?

Up to 2-4 times per day would be the ideal cadence. However, it's been found that if you have a Facebook following of 10,000 or more people, the number of clicks per post increases as you increase the frequency of your posts.

Say goodbye to juggling multiple platforms! With eCatholic's **Push to Facebook** feature, you can share news and blog posts straight from your website to your parish's Facebook page with just one click. It's a time-saver that helps extend your reach. And for those who aren't on social media? Your website ensures they still get the message—*no account required.*

Instagram, on the other hand, is all about visual storytelling. Share beautiful images of your church, inspiring memes, or behind-the-scenes glimpses of parish life through Instagram Stories. If you're feeling ambitious, Instagram Live is perfect for longer-form videos like short homilies or interviews. Otherwise, Reels are a great way to share short-form video content, like scriptural wisdom with Deacon John or Catechism 101 with Sister Mary in 60 seconds or less. In fact, Reels actually enable you to cast your digital "net" even wider, as they are not only delivered to your followers, but have the potential to be seen by any other unsuspecting swiper who may be searching for similar or related content. The power and reach of Instagram is often underestimated, so give it a try, give it some time, and watch the magic unfold.

How often should you post?
Instagram provides various avenues to post content—Posts, Reels, Stories, and Live. Here's our recommendations for each: **Posts & Reels** (1-3 times/day); **Stories** (2-4 times/day); **Live** (at least once per week). Ultimately, there is no limit to Instagram because the platform was designed for content to be consumed quickly.

X (formerly Twitter), moves at the speed of, well, a tweet! It's great for quick updates, joining broader Catholic conversations through Spaces (a feature for live conversations open to all users) or live-tweeting events. Imagine sharing real-time updates from your parish mission or Eucharistic Congress—it's like inviting the whole world to participate!

How often should you post?
Honestly, you can post as many times as you want on X. The key is not to disappear for extended periods of time as you can start to lose followers. Also, you may want to consider signing up for a Premium/Premium+ subscription which earns you the coveted Blue Checkmark and helps to broaden your reach on the platform. With either of these upgrades, you'll be able to compose messages beyond the 240 character limit, post longer video content, and even publish blog articles (Premium+ only).

Don't let its reputation for dance trends fool you—**TikTok** can be a powerful tool for reaching younger audiences with the Gospel message. Think of it as the modern-day parables: short, engaging stories that pack a spiritual punch. You could share quick Bible verse explanations or even "A Day in the Life of Father John" videos. And who knows? Perhaps your content might be what sets off the next viral trend!

How often should you post?
Typically, 1-3 times per day is ideal, but at a minimum, you should post at least once a day. Any momentum you've gained on the engagement front could affect future videos.

YouTube is a powerhouse for video content and can serve a wide range of purposes. From posting full homilies and educational series to sharing parish event highlights, YouTube allows you to create a comprehensive video library. Additionally, don't overlook the power of YouTube Shorts—short, bite-sized videos that are perfect for capturing attention quickly. Use **YouTube Shorts** to share snippets from sermons, quick inspirational messages, or fun, engaging content that can reach a broader audience. These short videos can be easily consumed and shared, helping you spread your message far and wide.

How often should you post?
If possible, at least 1 Short and 1 long-form video per day. It's recommended that you spread your videos apart by at least 1-2 hours. Posting a combination of Shorts and long-form videos each day will definitely help your channel grow much faster. Shorts will have a similar effect as Instagram Reels, since they are shorter and typically will catch the attention of some new followers.

But wait, there's more! Let's not forget about **LinkedIn**. While it might seem like an odd fit for ministry, LinkedIn can be a great platform for connecting with parishioners in their professional lives. Share content about living out your faith at work or Catholic social teaching. It's also a fantastic place to promote your parish's professional networking events or career ministry. Think of it as shining the light of Christ into the workplace!

How often should you post?
There's a lot of potential for organic reach on LinkedIn these days, so you could get away with posting just once per day. However, if you want to post 2 times a day, we'd recommend spacing your posts between 1-2 hours apart to allow time for your message to reach

your audience and stir up conversation. When it comes to the quality of your content, you'll want to make sure you pack sufficient value to make your followers come back for more.

> **KEY TAKEAWAYS**
>
> ⊙ **Platform-specific content**
> Tailor your content to fit the strengths of each platform (e.g., visual content for Instagram, short videos for TikTok, longer form content for Facebook, etc.).
>
> ⊙ **Consistency is key**
> Regular posting and engagement help build a strong online presence and keep your community connected. If you're feeling overwhelmed, don't spread yourself too thin. Pick one (maybe two) platform that you know you can contribute to regularly and do them well.
>
> ⊙ **Engage with followers**
> Respond to comments, messages, and interactions to foster a sense of community and show your followers that you care about what they have to say. After all, the goal of social media is to be, well...*social!*
>
> ⊙ **You don't have to be everywhere**
> We'll say it here, and we'll keep repeating it— you don't have to be on every platform. Choose the channels where your audience spends the majority of their time and focus all of your efforts on providing the best engagement experience for your followers.

Email & Text

Email might seem old school, but it's still one of the most effective ways to reach people directly. A weekly or monthly newsletter can keep your community informed about upcoming events, share resources, and highlight community news.

The true magic of email lies in list segmentation or "grouping." Just like tailoring announcements to different parish groups, sending targeted emails or texts to various segments of your community can make a world of difference. Different age groups and newcomers may have unique interests and needs, and grouping enables you to address these differences effectively.

When crafting your emails (or texts), keep in mind that most recipients will be reading on the go. The use of clear headers, short paragraphs, and a clean design is vital to ensure your messages are easy to digest. And always include a clear call to action—what do you want people to do after reading your email or text?

 With **eCatholic Connect**, you can easily manage your lists and create unlimited groups, craft beautiful, mobile-responsive messages, and send text messages for those urgent updates. It's like having a digital Swiss Army knife for all your communication needs! Visit **eCatholic.com/Connect**

KEY TAKEAWAYS

> **Send regularly**
> Send consistent email updates to keep your community informed, inspired, and engaged.

> **Personalization**
> Segment your lists to send targeted messages that are relevant to different groups in your parish. And try personalizing your messages by addressing each recipient by their name. Doing so will endear members to your community and make them feel more like part of the family.

> **Clear calls to action**
> Include clear instructions on what you want your members to do next, whether that's to sign up for an event or visit your website for more information.

Video & Live Streaming

In a world where everyone's carrying a video production studio in their pocket, video content has become a huge driver of engagement. It's a great way to make your message more engaging and personal. Getting started is not as difficult as you might think. Consider starting a YouTube channel for uploading long-form content like Sunday homilies or a pre-recorded faith formation series. Or, if you're feeling brave, dive into the world of short-form video on platforms like TikTok or Instagram. Imagine "Catechism Lessons in 60 Seconds with Father Tony"— a quick daily reflection that people can watch while waiting for their coffee to brew or to catch the bus. Short-form video has the potential to make the greatest impact.

And don't forget about live streaming, either. Streaming Masses and other special events allows those who can't attend in person to still feel part of the community. It's especially powerful for reaching the homebound or those who've moved away but still consider your parish their spiritual home. Also, don't stress about production quality. While, yes, we should all strive to achieve high-quality production, authenticity matters more than Hollywood-level polish.

KEY TAKEAWAYS

> **Provide engaging content**
> Use video to tell stories, share messages, and provide deeper insights into faith topics or addressing spiritual challenges we all face daily.

> **Live interaction**
> Besides live streaming Masses, explore new ways to interact in real-time with your community, offering Q&A sessions, bible studies or OCIA classes, concerts, and other live events.

> **Focus on authenticity**
> Prioritize authentic, heartfelt content over high production value. Viewers connect more with authentic, relatable messages than with polished but impersonal videos.

Think of it this way: by using these digital tools, you're not just adapting to the times—you're expanding your ministry's reach and potential in ways that St. Paul could have only dreamed of. So, take a deep breath, embrace the journey, and dive in! Over time, your content will take shape and you'll begin to adapt it to the way your community likes to be communicated with, and what you once thought was impossible will start making a difference in the lives of those you serve, one post, blog article, video, or message at a time.

Chapter 6
Multiply Your Message With Micro-Content

"Gather up the fragments so that nothing is lost."
— *John 6:12*

If your parish has ever hosted a beautiful retreat or powerful Lenten mission, you know how much effort, planning, and prayer go into making those moments meaningful. You book the speaker, promote the event, set up the space, and welcome attendees—hoping that the seeds planted will take root in people's lives. But here's a secret: the event itself is only the beginning. What if you could take the powerful content shared during a retreat or mission and multiply its impact far beyond the people who were able to attend in person?

That's where the concept of micro-content comes in. Simply put, it's the art of repurposing macro-content—like a retreat talk, testimony, or keynote presentation—into bite-sized, engaging content for your website, emails, and social media platforms.

From One To The Many

Let's say your parish hosted a two-night Lenten mission with a guest speaker. The talks were recorded and shared as full-length videos on your website. Instead of stopping there, here's how you could repurpose that same content across an entire week (or more):

- Clip short video highlights from key moments (30–90 seconds each) and share them as Reels, Shorts, or Stories on Instagram.

- Pull a quote from the speaker and create simple, branded graphics.

- Write a blog post summarizing one of the core themes with a reflection question at the end.

- Send a follow-up email to parishioners linking to a short recap or testimonial from someone who attended.

- Create a downloadable PDF of "5 Key Takeaways from Our Parish Mission" and promote it on your homepage.

- Share a volunteer spotlight or behind-the-scenes photo from the event prep as a way of highlighting parish life

- If you recorded or live streamed your parish mission or retreat on your website, make the recording available on-demand so those unable to attend in-person can go back and re-watch what they missed.

This isn't about creating more work. It's about extending the reach of something your parish already worked hard to produce. One night of content can become a full week—or month—of meaningful, faith-filled engagement online.

Why Micro-Content Is So Effective

Let's face it—your audience is busy. Not everyone can commit to a full retreat or mission, no matter how spiritually nourishing it is.

Micro-content makes deeper content more accessible by breaking it into smaller, more digestible pieces that can meet people where they are. It allows your community to engage with meaningful content on their own time, whether they're scrolling through social media on a lunch break or catching up on email in the evening. This approach also helps keep your online presence consistently active without the pressure of creating something entirely new every day. Most importantly, micro-content plants small seeds of faith—brief, thoughtful moments that can draw someone closer to the full message, or even inspire them to reconnect with your parish in a more meaningful way.

A Sample Weekly Plan

Here's what a week of micro-content might look like following a parish mission:

Day	Micro-Content Idea
Monday	Share a 3-minute video highlight with subtitles as a YouTube Short.
Tuesday	Post a meme or graphic quote with a key takeaway.
Wednesday	Publish a short blog post or reflection on the mission theme.
Thursday	Invite engagement with a striking clip from the mission and a question in your Instagram Stories (e.g., "What stuck with you from the mission?")
Friday	Share the full video link and a downloadable resource via email.
Saturday	Post a testimonial from someone who attended the mission in-person.

This strategy not only serves your online followers—it also builds anticipation for future events by showing your community that something powerful is always happening at your parish.

Divide and Conquer

You don't need to do this alone. Invite your parish

Screenshot of the Opus Clip interface. Used as an example of how eCatholic creates micro-content from each of its podcast episodes.

communications team, volunteers, or even parishioners to help generate content. Ask someone to take photos during the retreat. Invite a participant to share a short written reflection. Encourage a teen to clip a 30-second video from the recording using their phone.

Not everything has to be polished—it just has to be real. Authenticity connects far more deeply than perfection.

The goal of micro-content isn't just staying "on trend" or getting more likes. It's creating more entry points—little moments of grace that invite someone deeper into parish life and ultimately closer to Jesus.

Every time you repurpose content, you're helping "gather up the fragments" so that nothing is lost. And who knows? One short clip, quote, or image might be exactly what someone needed that day to reignite their faith.

Chapter 7
Turn Clicks Into Fellowship

"Encourage one another and build each other up, just as in fact you are doing." — 1 Thes. 5:11

So we've already covered the 'what' and 'where' of online ministry. Now it's time to dive into the 'how'. How do we turn our online presence into a thriving, engaged community? How do we make sure we're not just broadcasting into the void, but truly connecting with our members?

Roll Out the Digital 'Welcome Mat'

First things first, let's talk about fostering a welcoming online space. Think about how your parish wants a welcoming committee to greet new faces after Mass. Your online space needs the same warm, welcoming approach. Think of your website as your digital doorstep. Is it inviting? Easy to navigate?

Consider creating a "New Here?" page that's easy to find and filled with all the info a newcomer might need. It's like your virtual greeter, always ready with a smile and helpful information.

But a welcoming space is just the beginning. To truly build community, we need to encourage meaningful interactions. It's not enough to just post content and hope for the best. We need to spark conversations and create opportunities for real connections. Try asking thought-provoking questions in your content. "What does the Eucharist mean to you?" or "How do you live out your faith at work?" can lead to some amazing discussions.

Empower Your Community

And here's a key point to remember: your parishioners aren't just an audience – they're part of the team! Empowering your community to contribute is crucial for building a vibrant online presence. Consider featuring user-generated content, like testimonials or photos they've taken at parish events. It's like putting parishioners' artwork up in the church lobby – it shows that everyone's contribution is valued.

You could even start a community blog or vlog, inviting different ministry leaders or parishioners to contribute. This not only provides diverse, engaging content but also gives community members a sense of ownership and involvement in your online ministry.

But let's not forget that your online community doesn't exist in a vacuum. Finding ways to integrate your online and offline experiences is crucial. Promote online engagement during in-person events by encouraging people to share photos with a parish hashtag (e.g., #GetToMass) or to join online discussions about the event. Conversely, bring online discussions into real-world contexts. Use questions or topics from your online community as starting points for small group discussions or homilies. This cross-pollination helps create a seamless experience for your parishioners, whether they're interacting with your church online or in person.

And remember, building an engaged online community takes time and effort, but it's so worth it. You're not just accumulating followers; you're creating a space where people can encounter Christ and grow in their faith together.

 Pro Tip: *Consider starting your own podcast! It's a simple and powerful way to create engaging content that can be repurposed into blog posts, social media clips, and more. Best of all, getting started doesn't require a big budget—just a little creativity and a microphone. See **page 73** for tips on getting started, distribution, as well equipment recommendations.*

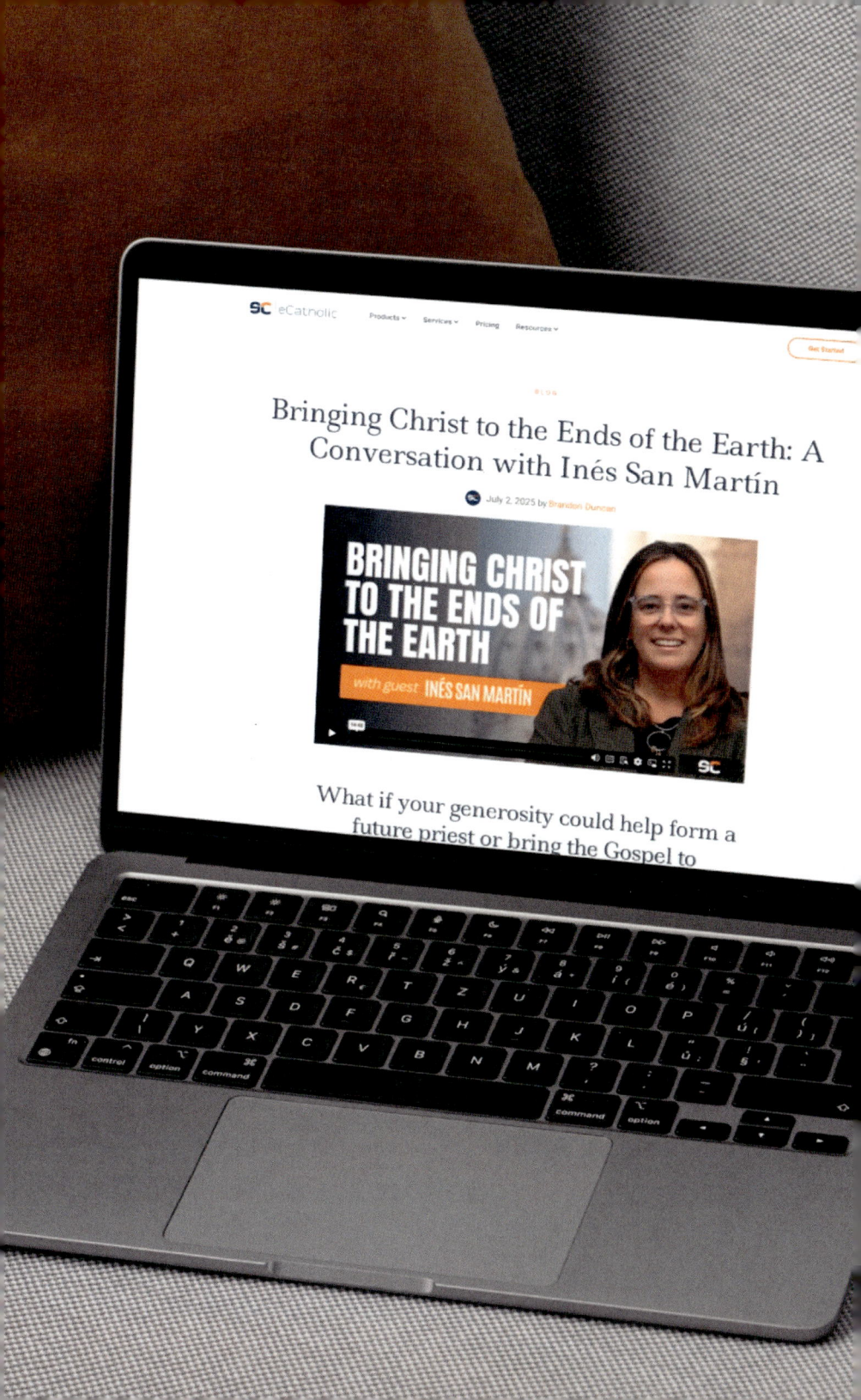

Chapter 8
Evaluating the Impact of Your Digital Ministry

"And let us not grow weary of doing good, for in due season we will reap, if we do not give up.." — Galatians 6:9

So, you've established your online presence, crafted some engaging content, and built a budding online community. Great work, but that's only the beginning! But how do you know if your efforts are really making an impact? Don't worry, we're not talking about counting 'Likes' for the sake of vanity metrics. This is about understanding how well we're spreading the Good News and connecting with our audiences.

Think of measuring your online messaging like taking the pulse of your parish. Just as you might look at Mass attendance or participation in ministries to gauge the health of your community, your online metrics can give you valuable insights into how well you're reaching and engaging people digitally.

Let's start with the basics. When we talk about measuring online messaging, we're looking at things like website traffic, social media engagement, email open rates, and video views. But keep in mind these numbers are just the starting point. The real goal is to understand the stories behind the stats. For example, let's say your parish website traffic has doubled in the past month. That's exciting! But the real questions are: What content is drawing people in? Are they finding what they need? Are they taking action, like signing up for events or ministries? These deeper insights can help you understand not just how many people you're reaching, but how effectively you're serving them.

Social media engagement is another key area to watch. But don't get too hung up on likes and follower counts. Instead, pay attention to comments, shares, and the quality of interactions. A thoughtful comment or a shared post can be far more valuable than a hundred passive likes. It shows that your content is resonating and inspiring action.

Google Analytics is a powerful, free tool that can provide valuable insights into your website's performance. This allows you to track your online traffic with ease, giving you a clear picture of how people are interacting with your site.

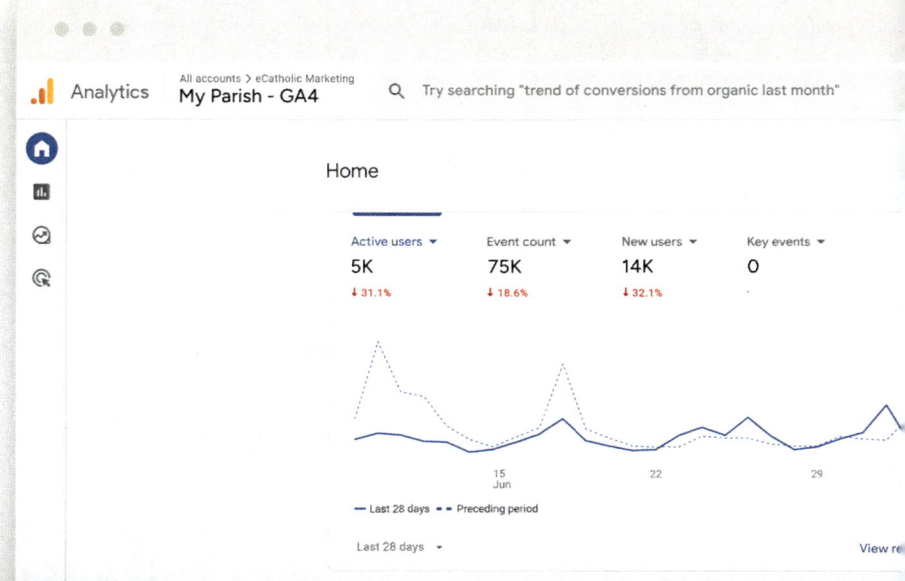

But gathering data is only half the battle. The real power comes from using these insights to improve your online ministry. Let's say you notice that your video reflections on Sunday's Gospel get a lot more engagement than your text posts. That's valuable information! It might suggest that your community responds well to visual content, or that they appreciate deeper dives into scripture. You could use this insight to create more video content or to develop a series of in-depth Gospel reflections, or maybe it might indicate to Father that an in-person event stemming from your online content might actually be a good idea.

Or perhaps you find that your website traffic spikes on Wednesday mornings. Armed with this knowledge, you could schedule your most important announcements or content for that time slot, ensuring they reach the maximum number of people.

The goal here isn't to chase numbers for their own sake. It's about understanding how to serve your community better and spread the Gospel more effectively. Every uptick in engagement represents a real person connecting with your message and potentially drawing closer to Christ. That's pretty amazing when it's put in that perspective!

Focus on what works

While it can be tempting to be everywhere at once, sometimes less is more. A strong presence on just a few platforms can be far more effective than spreading yourself thin across too many. Use your data to determine which channels are most effective for your parish community. For example, if Facebook and YouTube are where your audience is most engaged, focus your efforts there instead of trying to maintain a presence on less effective platforms.

Knowing the personas in your community—as discussed in the first chapter—can inform which platforms and content types will resonate most with different groups. By focusing on the channels that are most effective and most used by your community, you can avoid burnout and ensure your digital ministry is both sustainable and impactful.

In the end, it's about quality over quantity. A focused, intentional presence on the platforms that matter most to your community will do far more to further your mission than a scattered approach that tries to cater to every platform. Simply keep your eyes on the goal, which is to foster deeper connections with your parishioners, helping them grow in their faith, and leading them to an encounter with Jesus Christ.

You might be thinking, "I'm a pastor/ministry leader, not a data scientist!" Don't worry, you don't need a degree in statistics to measure your online impact effectively. The good news? eCatholic makes it easy to use Google Analytics with your website. Simply embed your Google Analytics code within the admin user settings of your eCatholic-powered website. Our support team can even help you get started!

Chapter 9
Navigating the Challenges of Evangelizing Online

*"Be strong and courageous. Do not be afraid;
do not be discouraged, for the Lord
your God will be with you wherever you go."*
— *Galatians 6:9*

Navigating the online terrain is not always smooth sailing. Just as the early Church faced challenges in spreading the Good News, we too can get bogged down and yet overcome the hurdles of the digital age.

Let's discuss some common challenges and how to tackle them with grace and creativity. In an era of instant communication and viral content, discussing sensitive issues requires careful consideration. Catholic organizations often need to address complex moral and social topics, which can be challenging in a fast-paced and often volatile online environment.

The key here is to approach these subjects with grace, clarity, and fidelity to Church teaching, while fostering constructive conversations. Consider establishing clear internal guidelines for how to handle controversial topics online. Train your team on these guidelines to ensure consistent messaging. Remember, the goal is to educate and inspire, not to engage in heated debates. There's plenty of bad news out there, we're here to be ambassadors for Christ and share his Good News!

When addressing sensitive issues, focus on providing resources and Church teachings rather than getting pulled into arguments. Use storytelling to illustrate Church positions on challenging issues. This approach can help make complex topics more relatable and easier to understand.

To give you an idea, here are some sample guidelines to consider when faced with having to address a difficult situation online:

> **Six Tips for Addressing Challenging Situations Online**
>
> 1. Always respond with compassion and respect, regardless of the viewpoint expressed.
>
> 2. Stick to official Church teachings and provide links to reputable Catholic resources for further reading.
>
> 3. Avoid engaging in arguments. Instead, invite private conversations by phone or in person with your pastor for more in-depth discussions.
>
> 4. Use "I/We" statements when possible, e.g., "As Catholics, we believe..." rather than "You're wrong about..."
>
> 5. If a comment violates your community guidelines (e.g., contains hate speech or personal attacks), hide or remove it, but consider reaching out privately to the individual if appropriate.

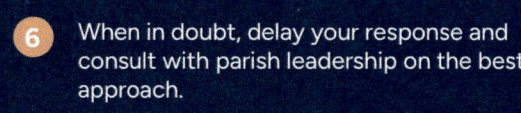

6. When in doubt, delay your response and consult with parish leadership on the best approach.

Always tailor your responses to your specific community context and consult with parish leadership on particularly sensitive issues. The goal is to communicate Church teaching clearly and compassionately, encourage conversation rather than debate, and always point people towards Christ and the Church's pastoral care.

Maintain a Consistent Voice Among All of Your Contributors

Many parishes and other Catholic organizations rely on a team of staff and volunteers to manage their online presence. While this collaborative approach can be a strength, it also presents the challenge of maintaining a consistent voice and message.

To tackle this, consider creating a style guide that outlines your organization's tone, voice, and key messages. Include examples of dos and don'ts for different platforms. This will help ensure your digital communications remain cohesive and aligned with your organization's mission, regardless of who's behind the keyboard.

Implementing a content approval process can also be helpful. Set up a system for reviewing and approving posts before they go live. Tools like content calendars can help you plan and coordinate messaging across your team.

Change is a Constant in the Digital Age

The digital landscape is constantly evolving, with new platforms and tools emerging all the time. Keeping up can feel overwhelming, especially for busy ministry leaders who already wear multiple hats.

The key here is to focus on the fundamentals rather than chasing every new trend. Prioritize platforms where your community is most active. It's better to have a strong presence on one or two platforms than a weak presence on many.

Stay informed about digital trends, but don't feel pressured to adopt every new technology. Instead, evaluate new tools based on how well they align with your ministry goals and your community's needs. It certainly doesn't hurt to learn about and experiment with new apps; however, the latest app or social media platform is just a tool – your message and your connection with your community are what truly matter.

Measuring Success in Ministry Terms

As mentioned in the previous chapter, it's easy to get caught up in metrics (e.g., likes, shares, and follower counts). But as ministry leaders, we need to measure success in terms that align with our mission, which is the mission of the Church: to lead souls to Christ.

Instead of focusing solely on quantity, consider the quality of your community's engagement. Are people sharing meaningful reflections in your comment sections? Are you seeing increased participation in parish life as a result of your online efforts? Are you reaching people who might not otherwise connect with your parish?

One heartfelt comment or one person drawn closer to Christ is worth more than a thousand passive likes. Keep your focus on the impact you're making in people's lives and faith journeys.

Every challenge is an opportunity to innovate and better serve your community. By addressing these common hurdles head-on, you'll be well-equipped to create an engaging online presence that truly reflects the heart of Jesus to all who encounter you online.

Chapter 10
Where Do We Go From Here?

*"Your word is a lamp for my feet,
a light on my path"* — *Psalm 119:105*

Well, we've come to the end of this journey, but really, this is only the beginning of your adventure in digital ministry. Let's take a moment to reflect on what we've covered and look ahead to the amazing possibilities that await you.

We've explored a lot together, from understanding your audiences to crafting engaging content, building vibrant communities, and navigating the sometimes choppy waters of managing online communities. But now comes the exciting part–putting all of this into action! But don't feel like you need to overhaul your entire online presence overnight. Start small, be consistent, and gradually build your digital ministry. Consider performing an audit of your online presence and discern whether to expand or cut any outlets that may or may not be proving fruitful.

Again, your online presence isn't just about likes, shares, or follower counts. It's about extending your ministry, reaching souls, and spreading the Good News of Jesus to all who will listen. Every post, tweet, or video is an opportunity to touch someone's life, to offer hope, to invite someone to a deeper encounter with the Catholic faith.

You're not just managing websites, live streams, and social media accounts – you're creating digital doorways that can lead people to an encounter with Christ and His Church. If you're feeling a bit overwhelmed, take a deep breath. Remember, the apostles didn't have a social media strategy when they set out from Galilee to spread the Gospel, but they changed the world. You have the same mission, just with some nifty new tools at your disposal.

Don't be afraid to start small, learn as you go, and yes, even make mistakes. The digital world can be forgiving at times, and your community will appreciate your authentic efforts to connect and engage. And don't forget to refer back to this guide if you get stuck and need some faithful reminders.

So, where do you go from here? Plan, plan, and plan. Planning your content in advance will keep you accountable to your online community and ensure that the content you share aligns with your mission. Do everything with intentionality and purpose. Perhaps it's creating that "Welcome" video for your website, or maybe it's starting a weekly "Ask Father" feature on one of your social channels. Whatever it is, approach it with enthusiasm, creativity, and, of course, always with prayer. In the wisdom of St. Francis de Sales, "Every morning prepare your soul for a tranquil day." This reminds us to begin every task with prayer, inviting God's guidance and peace into our work. By doing so, we transform our efforts into acts of faith and love toward God as he creates opportunities for us to evangelize and bring souls to him.

Be confident; you're not alone in this journey. There's a whole community of Catholic communicators and influencers out there, learning and growing together. Don't hesitate to reach out, share ideas, and support one another.

Your online community is waiting, and the digital mission field is ripe for the harvest. Trust the Holy Spirit to guide you, and watch in awe as God works through your efforts to touch hearts and change lives as only He can.

To Him be the glory! +

Resources

Here's a curated list of practical tools that every parish communications team should know about. While there may be a small learning curve at first, many of these tools are surprisingly easy to use, budget-friendly (some even free), and perfectly suited for creating the kinds of content parishes need most—like flyers, bulletin inserts, social media posts, videos, music, and more.

Graphic Design

Canva
- *Best for:* Flyers, social media graphics, posters, bulletins
- Teams can collaborate in real-time
- Includes access to stock photos, graphics, and even video.
- Available for free to non-profits; application required on their website)

Adobe Express
- *Best for:* Quick designs and brand control
- Great alternative to Canva with Adobe's design power
- Easily create branded social graphics, posters, and videos.

Figma
- *Best for:* Collaborative design with advanced flexibility
- Excellent for teams used to Adobe tools (e.g., Photoshop/Illustrator)

Stock Photos & Catholic Imagery

eCatholic Stock Photos (included with your eCatholic-powered website)
CathoPic (cathopic.com)
Catholic Stock (catholicstock.com)
Pexels (pexels.com)
Unsplash (unsplash.com)

Typography & Fonts

Google Fonts (fonts.google.com)
FontPair (fontpair.co)

Image Editing & Customization

Pixlr (pixlr.com)
- *Why it's great:* Free, browser-based Photoshop alternative
- *Use it for:* Quick edits, overlays, retouching photos

Remove.bg (remove.bg)
- *Why it's great:* Automatically removes image backgrounds, which can also be done in Canva, Adobe Express, and Figma.

Video Editing Tools

iMovie (Mac/iOS)
- *Why it's great:* Free, beginner-friendly, good for quick promo or reflection videos.

Adobe Premiere Rush/Premiere Pro
- **Rush:** Fast, simplified mobile/desktop tool for quick edits
- **Pro:** Industry-standard software for advanced user

DaVinci Resolve
- *Why it's great:* Free professional-grade tool with color correction and audio editing

AI-Powered Video Editing Tools

Descript (descript.com)
- *Why it's great:* Edit video like a Word doc. Automatically generates transcripts, removes filler words, and lets you drag & drop edits.

VEED.IO (veed.io)
- *Why it's great:* Easy online editor with auto-subtitles, brand kits, and video resizing for all platforms.
- *Use it for:* Making sermon clips social-media ready in minutes.

CapCut (capcut.com)
- *Why it's great:* Free (from ByteDance, the TikTok parent company), great mobile tool with templates, transitions, and auto-captions
- *Use it for:* Youth ministry content, quick reels, Instagram Stories or YouTube Shorts.

Submagic (submagic.co)
- *Use it for:* Sermon snippets, youth reels, or devotionals with punchy subtitles.

Opus Clip (opus.pro)
- *Why it's great:* Turn long-form videos into viral-ready short clips.
- *Use it for:* Youth ministry content, quick reels, Instagram Stories or YouTube Shorts.

AI-Powered Music Generation Tools

Riffusion (riffusion.com)
- A music generator that uses diffusion models (similar to how AI generates images) to create original music–often in real time–based on text prompts.
- Free and premium subscriptions available; royalty free for commerical use with a premium level subcription.

Loudly (loudly.com/music)
- Create or download curated AI-generated music
- Personal and commercial use license included with a paid subscription.

Starting Your Own Podcast

Launching a podcast might sound intimidating, but with the right tools, it's easier than you think. Whether you're looking to share homilies, record spiritual reflections, highlight stories from your parish, or produce a whole new show, podcasting is a powerful way to evangelize in the digital world.

Here are some tools and resources to help you get started:

Recording & Editing Tools

These tools help you capture great audio and make simple edits–even if you're brand new to audio production.

Audacity (audacityteam.com)
- Free, open-source audio editor that works on Mac or PC. Great for beginners.

GarageBand (Mac only)
- Pre-installed on Macs and perfect for recording and editing audio with minimal fuss.

Descript (descript.com)
- AI-powered editor that lets you edit audio by editing the transcript–great for teams who prefer working with text.

Riverside.fm (riverside.fm)
- A great tool for recording remote interview in high quality. Especially useful if you plan to interview guests from outside your parish.

StreamYard (streamyard.com)
- Another powerful recording and editing tool for video and audio podcasts. Especially helpful for conducting remote video/audio interviews. Can be a little pricey, but completely worth the investment if you're doing to dive in!

Microphone Recommendations

- **Blue Yeti:** Affordable, east-to-use USB mic with great sound quality ($100+)
- **RØDE PodMic:** Compact, professional sound in a small package ($100)
- **Shure SM7B/SM7dB:** High-quality, professional grade microphone for the serious podcaster ($400-$500)

Podcast Hosting Platforms

A podcast needs a home–this is where your audio files live and where directories like Apple or Spotify pull your episodes from.

Spotify for Creators (creators.spotify.com)*
- This free platform makes it easy to record, host, and distribute your podcast directly to Spotify and other platforms. Great for beginners.

Buzzsprout (buzzsprout.com)
- Known for its easy-to-use dashboard and helpful analytics. Offers a free plan with paid upgrades.

Podbean (podbean.com)
- Offers hosting, distribution, and even a simple podcast website. Good balance of tools and pricing.

Distribute Your Podcast

Once you've uploaded your episodes to a host, make sure to distribute them to all the major listening platforms, including:

- Spotify
- Apple Podcasts
- Amazon Music
- iHeartRadio

Each hosting provider has their way of submitting your show to be syndicated on their platform, so be sure to follow the instructions provided by your host.

Behind the Scenes of The Engaged Parish Podcast

As a fully remote team, we needed a setup that would make recording our podcast easy—no matter where our guests are located. Here's a quick look at the tools we use to record and produce each episode of *The Engaged Parish Podcast*.

We use **StreamYard** to record all our interviews. It's browser-based, user-friendly, and perfect for remote setups. Our guests can join from anywhere in the country with just a link. StreamYard records each session both in the cloud and locally on each participant's computer, so we never have to worry about losing footage.

After recording, we can download high-quality audio and video files—plus a full transcript, which helps us quickly write the summary blog post for our website.

For a little post-production polish, we turn to **Adobe Podcast** (podcast.adobe.com)—especially helpful when we need to remove background noise or level out inconsistent audio. Just upload your file and let Adobe work its magic. (*Note: Free Adobe account required.*)

For recording, we use the **Shure SM7B**, a studio-quality microphone that captures clear, rich sound. It's connected to our laptop via the **Elgato Wave XLR**, a compact audio interface that lets us control mic gain, headphone volume, and monitoring levels—all with a single dial. Any wired headphones plug right in for easy monitoring.

To keep things simple and adjustable, we mount the mic on an **Elgato Wave Mic Arm LP**, a low-profile boom arm that attaches to our desk. It keeps the mic comfortably positioned while recording and tucks away easily when not in use.

Since *The Engaged Parish Podcast* is also a video podcast, we use the **Elgato FaceCam Pro**, a high-quality webcam that delivers sharp, professional-looking video without needing a full camera rig.

Recording while on the road? Here's what we use: When we're recording outside the office—like at conferences or on-site interviews—we bring along the **RØDECaster Pro II**. It's an all-in-one sound mixer that lets us plug in our microphones and headphones, adjust audio levels, and record everything from a single, easy-to-use interface. It makes high-quality, on-the-go podcasting simple and stress-free.

Rode also makes a smaller, more affordable version of our sound mixer in the **RØDECaster Duo**.

And that's our setup!

If you enjoyed the contents of this book, please reach out and let us know at **hello@ecatholic.com**. We'd love to hear from you!

Made in the USA
Coppell, TX
18 January 2026